Digging deep

Building the first underground railway meant lots of hard digging. Workers used shovels to dig out the earth. It was lifted to the surface in baskets.

⑥ workers building High Street Kensington station, about 1868

The Train Under Your Feet

Contents

Our crowded cities	2	Moles in the clay	14
Pollution on four legs	4	Not just digging	16
Digging deep	6	Not just for trains	18
From steam to electric	8	Glossary	20
A web of lines	10	Index	21
Tunnelling the world	12	Underground networks	22

Written by Richard Platt

Our crowded cities

We live in a crowded world. Cars, buses and trucks make the roads very busy. In big cities, traffic would stop if we didn't have tunnels underground. **Passengers** can use fast **subway trains** under their feet.

Did you know?
More than a billion cars are being used in the world.

Pollution on four legs

Underground railways were first built in London 150 years ago. There were no cars then. Horses pulled passengers and **cargo**. But travelling this way was as slow as walking and left behind a smelly problem!

traffic in London in the 19th century

The world's first subway was finished in just two years. It was called the Metropolitan Railway and was six kilometres long. It linked London's main railway stations to the **business** district.

King's Cross underground station, on the Metropolitan Railway, around 1865

From steam to electric

Steam trains pulled the **carriages**. They filled the tunnels with smoke and **soot**. **Engineers** tried to make the tunnels less dirty and stuffy by adding chimneys. This helped, but didn't fix the problem.

a steam train pulling into a station

Electric power replaced steam in 1890. The electric trains were fast, clean and fairly quiet.

an electric train, about 1906

A web of lines

More underground railways were built in London, crossing the city's centre. Outside the centre, trains rose out of the tunnels above ground. By 1930 there were 205 kilometres of track.

a map of the London Underground in 1933

children get on the train at Eastcote in London, 1925

Tunnelling the world

Large cities such as Budapest, Boston and Paris built subway systems too.

In 1900 work began on New York's first subway. It took more than four years to complete. Since then, 200 kilometres of tunnels have been added.

passengers riding on a special open car on the day the New York subway opened

New York has one of the biggest subway systems in the world.

Did you know?
Trains make over 7,800 trips on the New York subway every day.

the New York subway today

Moles in the clay

The building of subways changed. Shovels and baskets were no use deep underground. From 1887, engineers worked on London's Underground with tunnelling machines called moles.

Today, these moles use huge spinning cutters. They can dig over 60 centimetres of tunnel every hour.

a mole cutting a tunnel in California, USA

Not just digging

Digging a tunnel is just the beginning. Running a subway system is a difficult job. More than three million Londoners rely on the Underground to get to work every day. Computers are used to make sure the trains arrive on time. Workers clean and repair the trains and track.

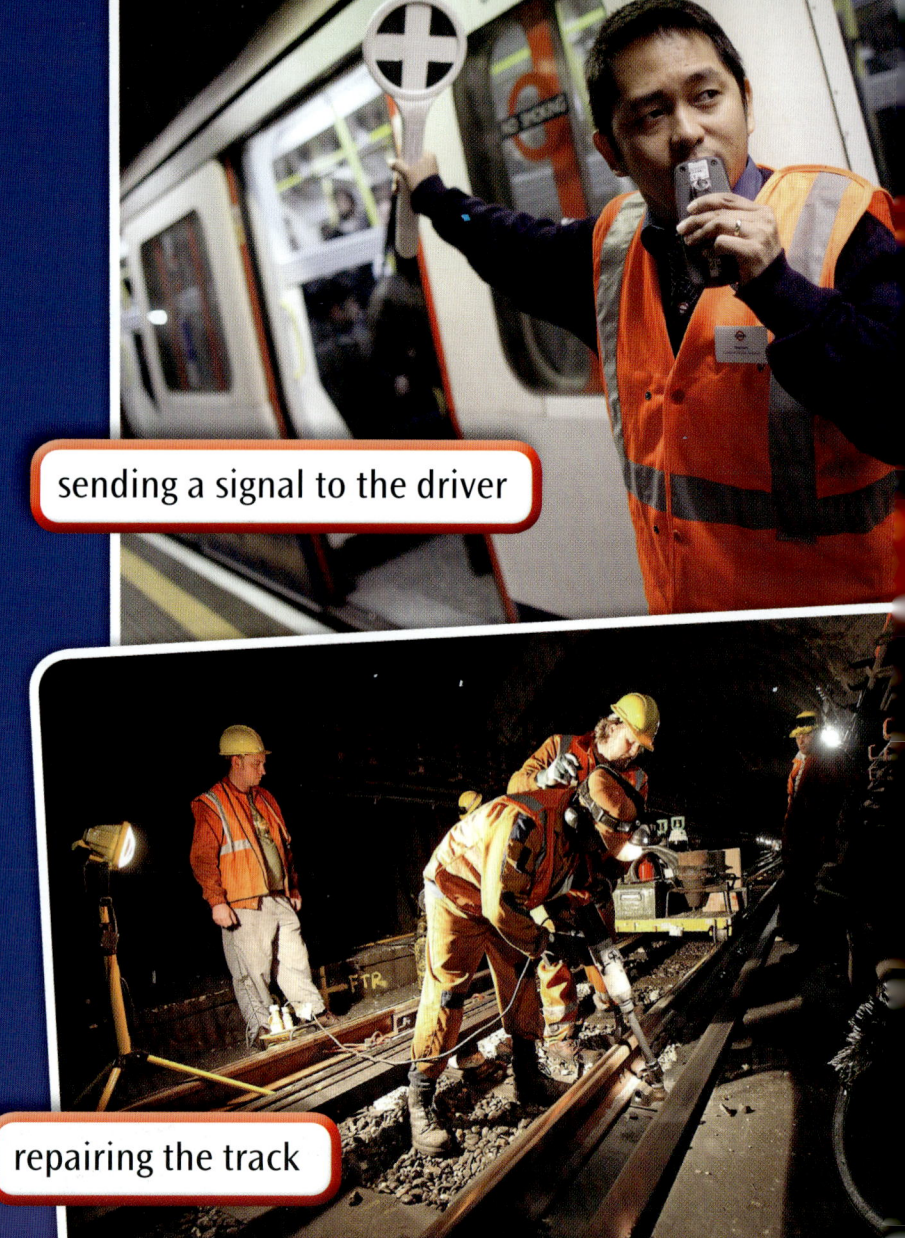

sending a signal to the driver

repairing the track

driving a train

watching the platforms

sweeping the platform

Not just for trains

Subway tunnels have been used to keep people safe from danger.

During World War II, people used the London Underground to escape the bombs.

Aldwych station was closed in 1994.

Some tunnels and stations are closed down when there aren't enough passengers using them. Most of these stations are empty. But London's Aldwych station has been used in films and TV programmes.

Glossary

business	making, buying or selling goods or services for money
cargo	goods transported by vehicles
carriage	a part of the train for passengers
engineers	people who design roads, engines, railways and other things
passengers	people that travel in or on a vehicle
pollution	making the air, water or soil dirty
soot	black powder that is made when wood or coal is burnt
subway trains	trains that are underground

Index

building railways   6, 14

cars   2, 4

computers   16

digging   6, 16

driving trains   17

electric trains   9

horses   4

London Underground   4, 7, 8, 10, 11, 16–17, 18–19

London Underground map   10

Metropolitan Railway   7

moles   14–15

New York subway   12–13

pollution   4

repairs   16

steam trains   8

traffic   2–3, 4

tunnels   2, 8, 10, 12, 15, 18, 19

World War II   18

Underground railways over time

22

23

Ideas for reading

Written by Gillian Howell
Primary Literacy Consultant

Learning objectives: *(reading objectives correspond with Turquoise band; all other objectives correspond with Ruby band)* read independently and with increasing fluency longer and less familiar texts; use knowledge of different organisational features of texts to find information effectively

Curriculum links: History, Geography

Interest words: underground, pollution, passengers, surface, Metropolitan, stations, business, carriages, engineers, systems

Resources: pens, paper, internet, whiteboard

Word count: 496

Getting started

- Read the title and blurb with the children and discuss the cover photo. Ask them if they have ever travelled on an underground train and what it was like. Ask them what benefits they think there are to travelling underground compared to travelling above ground and write their ideas on the whiteboard.

- Turn to the contents page and read the headings together. Ask the children if they think the book should be read in sequence or dipped into. Elicit that it is better to read the information in sequence because it is about the history of the underground.

Reading and responding

- Turn to p2 and read the page together to familiarise the children with the structure and features of the book. Ask the children to say why certain words are in bold print and to find them in the glossary. Read the glossary entries together to pre-empt any difficulties and enable children to read the text more fluently.

- Ask the children to find the *Did you know?* box on p2. Ask them to say why they think the information in the box is separate from the main text.

- Ask the children to read the book and, as they read, find and note down three interesting facts to explain to the rest of the group later. Listen in as they read and prompt when children struggle with any words.